HOOPS HEROES

The Untold Story of Black Basketball

Elliott Smith
Cicely Lewis, Executive Editor

Lerner Publications ◆ Minneapolis

LETTER FROM CICELY LEWIS

Dear Reader,

When you think of today's star Black athletes, who comes to mind? Maybe you think of LeBron James, Mookie Betts, Dak Prescott, or Simone Biles. They are all great athletes. But do you know who paved the way for them?

Cicely Lewis

I began Read Woke Books to challenge social norms and to share stories of people from underrepresented and oppressed groups. In this series, you will be introduced to lesser-known athletes and the barriers they overcame to make great changes in sports.

Sports is more than a game. Throughout history, sports have been a way to help fight injustices in our world. As you read, think about how the actions athletes have made in their sports have impacted the world.

I hope these books inspire you to never give up. Someone has to take the first step, and it might as well be you.

Power to the Reader,

Cicely Lewis, Executive Editor

TABLE OF CONTENTS

KING OF THE COURT **4**

CHAPTER 1
A NEW GAME. **6**

CHAPTER 2
SPREAD THE WORD **12**

CHAPTER 3
BRIGHT STARS **16**

CHAPTER 4
LASTING LEGACY **20**

Glossary. 28
Source Notes 29
Read Woke Reading List 30
Index 31

The New York Renaissance play against the Minneapolis Lakers on April 11, 1948.

KING OF THE COURT

Black people have not always been allowed to play sports alongside white athletes. Instead, Black people had to create their own leagues and teams. For basketball, Black people created the Black Fives. The teams were made up of Black players, with five from each team on the court at one time.

One of the biggest stars of the Black Fives Era was Charles "Tarzan" Cooper. Cooper was a center. He excelled at grabbing rebounds and passing. In 1929 he joined the New York

Charles "Tarzan" Cooper of the New York Renaissance

Renaissance (Rens)—then the most successful Black Fives team.

Cooper helped the Rens win 88 straight games in 1932–1933. During his 11 years with the Rens, the team won 1,303 of 1,506 games.

In 1977 Cooper became the first Black player to join the Naismith Memorial Basketball Hall of Fame. But many of his accomplishments, along with those of the Black Fives Era's other stars, have faded with time.

Black Fives players helped pave the way for the Black high school, college, National Basketball Association (NBA), and Women's National Basketball Association (WNBA) stars. They have a huge role in basketball history.

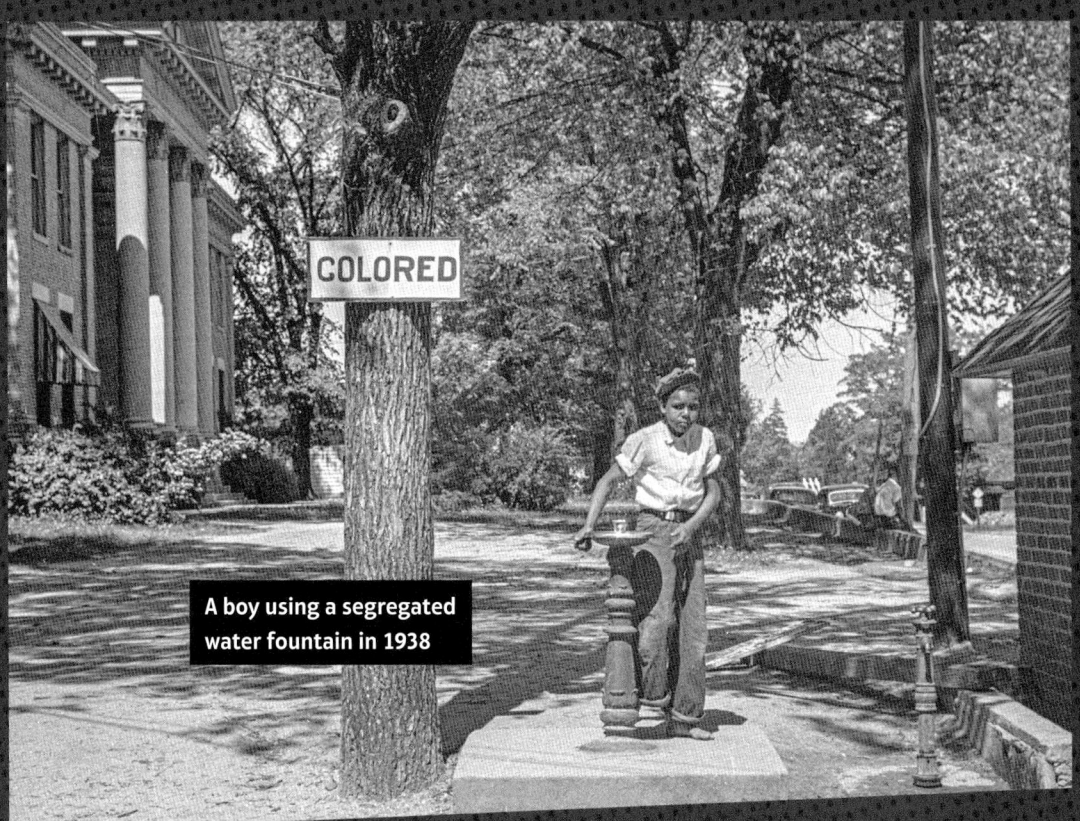

A boy using a segregated water fountain in 1938

CHAPTER 1
A NEW GAME

Throughout the 1800s and 1900s, much of the US was segregated. Black people were not allowed to go to the same places as white people, such as schools and movie theaters. And they were not allowed to play on the same sports teams.

Physical education teacher James Naismith invented basketball in 1891 in Springfield, Massachusetts. The game quickly became popular. Edwin B. Henderson, another physical education teacher, learned the game in its early years.

James Naismith was the inventor of basketball.

Henderson took summer session classes at Harvard University. There, he learned the rules of basketball. He brought the game back to Washington, DC. In 1904 he began teaching the sport to Black male students at segregated schools. Henderson also played, often as a center.

In the early 1900s, Henderson formed the Interscholastic Athletic Association, an amateur

Edwin B. Henderson, 1912

Edwin B. Henderson (*front, center*) and other members of the 12th Street YMCA team in 1910

sports conference for Black high school and college athletes. Henderson's 12th Street YMCA team was one of the best teams. They played against teams from Maryland, Pennsylvania, and New York. In 1909–1910 the undefeated team won the title of Colored Basketball World Champions.

REFLECT

These early basketball teams played for the Colored Basketball World Championship. How were outdated terms for Black people such as *colored* and Negro used to lessen the accomplishments of these athletes?

> "Without [Henderson] who knows if [basketball] ever would have been embraced as it was."
>
> —Claude Johnson, author, 2008

In 1910 Henderson convinced Howard University to make the 12th Street team its varsity program since most of the players were students at the school. The team won the national championship once again with Henderson as coach.

Henderson helped Howard University start a varsity basketball team in 1910.

DID YOU KNOW?

Henderson is known as the Father and Grandfather of Black Basketball. He joined the Naismith Memorial Basketball Hall of Fame in 2013.

Henderson's grandson Edwin Henderson II (*second from left*) attends the 2013 ceremony for the Naismith Memorial Basketball Hall of Fame.

A 1946 basketball team in Wilkinsburg, Pennsylvania

Henderson continued to teach and promote basketball for years. He believed that basketball was an activity for everyone.

Women had been playing the sport since 1892. But it would take several more years for women's leagues to form.

The Smart Set of Brooklyn in 1910

CHAPTER 2
SPREAD THE WORD

From its small beginnings, basketball spread across the country. The first men's all-Black teams formed in 1906 in New York City. They played other amateur teams from around the area in small tournaments.

In 1907 the Smart Set of Brooklyn played the Crescent Athletic Club in Washington, DC. It was the first game between Black teams from different cities.

The first women Black Fives teams started in 1910. The New York Girls, the Spartan Girls of Brooklyn, and the Jersey Girls were rivals. On February 26, 1910, the New York Girls and the Jersey Girls met in the first recorded game between two Black women's teams.

Other women's teams formed as far away as Kansas. Black newspapers around the country covered the teams' players and games.

This March 1934 newspaper includes an article about basketball.

Before long, bigger options arose for Black Fives teams. In 1922 the Commonwealth Big Five became the first all-Black pro team. The New York Rens were founded the next year. Pro teams took on all opponents. They played both Black and white teams.

Many Black teams could not play at gyms and athletic clubs that allowed only white people. Black Fives games were often held in ballrooms, church basements, or armories. There was usually a dance after the game. Teams barnstormed across the country, traveling by bus to compete for the title of Colored Basketball World Champions.

From game to game, the rules could even change. In the South, women's teams were made up of six players, three on offense and three on defense. Some of those teams were called Black Sixes.

REFLECT

Black newspapers often covered Black Fives games, while white newspapers largely ignored the games. How do you think this had a long-term effect on these players and their role in basketball history?

DID YOU KNOW?

The Harlem Globetrotters got their start as a Black Fives team. They spent years barnstorming before developing into their skilled comedy and hoops act.

Members of the Harlem Globetrotters 1931 basketball team

Cumberland Posey Jr. (*standing, left*) played in the Black Fives and also was a player and manager in the Negro Leagues. Here, he poses with the 1930 Negro League team Homestead Grays.

CHAPTER 3
BRIGHT STARS

The heroes of the Black Fives Era have largely been lost to time. But these talented players were important in the game's growth. They showed talent in a newer sport during an era of racism and segregation.

Cumberland Posey Jr. was one of the earliest stars. Posey was a natural athlete of multiple sports. He played basketball in high school in Pittsburgh, Pennsylvania. Then he became the first Black basketball player at Penn State in 1909.

Every year from 1920 to 1923, Posey won the Colored

Ora Washington in 1939

Basketball World Championship. He is the only person in the Halls of Fame for both basketball and baseball.

Ora Washington was another star of multiple sports. She excelled at tennis, winning the singles championships seven years in a row in a Black tennis league. But then she added basketball to her résumé.

Beginning in 1932, Washington played center for the Philadelphia Tribune Girls. She helped them win 11 straight championships thanks to her scoring and defense. She joined the Women's Basketball Hall of Fame in 2009 and the Naismith Memorial Basketball Hall of Fame in 2018.

The New York Rens became a pro Black basketball team in 1923.

REFLECT

In what ways do you think Black Fives stars such as Washington and Posey changed basketball? How are these changes a part of basketball today?

DID YOU KNOW?

In 1925 the Roamer Girls joined the Chicago City Basketball League. In the league, Black and white teams of all genders played against one another.

Clarence "Fats" Jenkins became a member of the New York Rens in 1923. The lightning-fast guard was the team's captain for 15 years.

In the early days of basketball, a jump ball took place at center court after every basket. Even though Jenkins was one of the Rens's smaller players, his leaping skills made him the team's choice to jump center.

Isadore Channels played for the Roamer Girls in Chicago throughout the 1920s and 1930s. She was known for her shooting. In a 1925 game against the Harvey Bloomers, a white team, Channels scored 19 points. The Roamer Girls won the game 29–3.

> "She played a game far above the heads of her opponents and far in advance of her colleagues."
>
> —Chicago Defender, Isadore Channels article, 1925

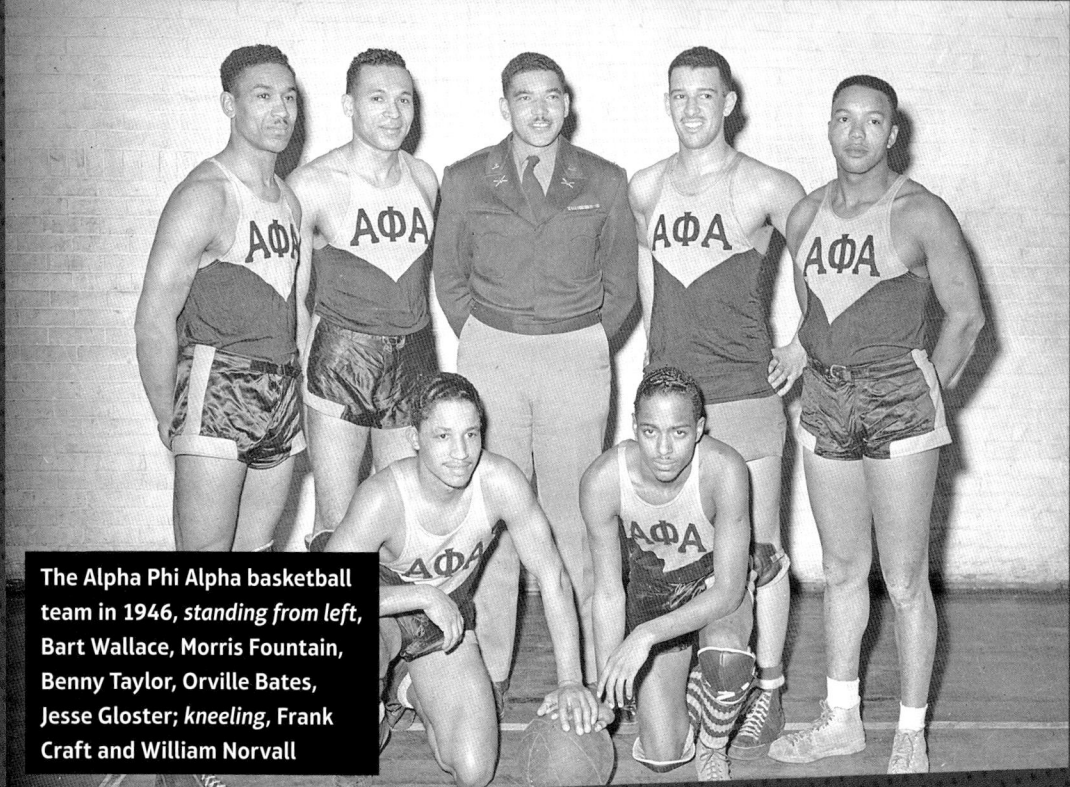

The Alpha Phi Alpha basketball team in 1946, *standing from left*, Bart Wallace, Morris Fountain, Benny Taylor, Orville Bates, Jesse Gloster; *kneeling*, Frank Craft and William Norvall

CHAPTER 4
LASTING LEGACY

Throughout the 1930s, Black players were becoming more common on college basketball teams. They played for Historically Black Colleges and Universities such as Xavier University of Louisiana and Bennett College.

Major college programs began adding Black players. Jackie Robinson played on the basketball court for the University of California, Los Angeles, before becoming the first Black player in pro baseball. In 1948 Don Barksdale became the first Black player to win an Olympic gold medal in basketball.

Jackie Robinson playing for UCLA in 1939

Don Barksdale playing for the Boston Celtics in 1953

Black Fives teams were still around. But slowly, basketball began to integrate. In 1942 the National Basketball League added 10 Black players to two teams. In 1946 the Basketball Association of America formed. It merged with the National Basketball League in 1949 to form the NBA.

In the 1950–1951 season, three Black men joined the NBA. Chuck Cooper of the Harlem Globetrotters was the first Black player drafted by an NBA team. Nat "Sweetwater" Clifton of the New York Rens was the first Black player to sign a contract. And Earl Lloyd was the first Black person to play in an NBA game.

REFLECT

Every year on April 15, Major League Baseball has a special day for Jackie Robinson, the first Black player in the league. How could the NBA and WNBA have a special day for Black Fives heroes?

The Black Fives Era ended as the NBA integrated. Many Black Fives teams stopped playing. Others, like the Globetrotters, barnstormed, but not for long. The door closed for women players. Many Black women played in college, but pro options were slim for all women athletes for many years.

Nat "Sweetwater" Clifton grabs a rebound during a 1952 game.

Leroy Ellis (*number 25*) and Mel Counts (*number 11*) reach for a rebound during a 1965 NBA game.

Trish Roberts (*holding the ball*) plays for Team USA in the 1976 Olympics.

In 1976 women's basketball was added to the Olympics. Then, in 1978, the Women's Professional Basketball League formed. But the league ended in 1981. Finally, in 1997, the WNBA formed and began play.

DID YOU KNOW?

Lusia Harris is the only woman ever selected in the NBA Draft. In 1992 she was the first Black woman to join the Naismith Memorial Basketball Hall of Fame.

Lusia Harris shoots a layup during a 1977 game.

The WNBA's Minnesota Lynx play against the Chicago Sky in 2023.

Russell Westbrook dribbles the ball during a game in 2023.

For years, many basketball fans have forgotten the Black Fives Era. In 2013 the Black Fives Foundation formed. Its mission is to honor the pre-NBA and pre-WNBA history of Black people in basketball. Modern teams and players have also begun to acknowledge and recognize the importance of the Black Fives Era.

"These teams helped break racial and societal barriers and paved the way for the game and the NBA as a whole," NBA star Russell Westbrook said.

GLOSSARY

amateur: someone who takes part in an activity or sport without pay

armory: a large storage area for war equipment

barnstorm: to travel through the country making brief stops for games

conference: a group of teams that play one another

draft: a yearly event where teams take turns choosing new players

integrate: to make a place for or job open to all racial and ethnic groups

merge: to bring two or more separate units or organizations into one unit

rival: a person or group in competition with another person or group

segregation: a legal system of forced separation, done specifically by race

varsity: the main team representing a high school or college

SOURCE NOTES

9   David L. Tannenwald, "The Grandfather of Black Basketball," *Harvard Magazine*, December 15, 2022, https://www.harvardmagazine.com/2022/12/edwin-bancroft-henderson-the-grandfather-of-black-basketball.

19 Robert Pruter, "Isadore Channels and the Roamer Girls: A Great African American Basketball and Tennis Star," *The World of Amateur & Youth Sports in Chicago* (blog), June 27, 2019, https://historyofsport.wordpress.com/2019/06/27/isadore-channels-and-the-roamer-girls-a-great-african-american-basketball-and-tennis-star-essay-by-robert-pruter/.

27 Nellie Andreeva and Denise Petski, "Black Fives Era Documentary in Works from NBA's Russell Westbrook & Propagate," Deadline, January 4, 2022, https://deadline.com/2022/01/black-fives-era-documentary-nba-russell-westbrook-propagate-black-fives-foundation-1234904202/.

READ WOKE READING LIST

Black Fives Foundation
https://www.blackfives.org

Britannica Kids: National Basketball Association (NBA)
https://kids.britannica.com/students/article/National-Basketball-Association-NBA/624441

Kiddle: Black Fives Facts for Kids
https://kids.kiddle.co/Black_Fives

Moore, Madison. *More Than Just a Game: The Black Origins of Basketball*. Chicago: Albert Whitman, 2021.

Slade, Suzanne. *Swish! The Slam-Dunking, Alley-Ooping, High-Flying Harlem Globetrotters*. New York: Little, Brown, 2020.

Smith, Elliott. *Ballpark Legends: The Legacy of the Negro Leagues*. Minneapolis: Lerner Publications, 2025.

Sports Illustrated Kids: Black Fives Basketball
https://www.sikids.com/from-the-mag/hidden-hard-court-heroes

WNBA: History
https://www.wnba.com/history

INDEX

Channels, Isadore, 19
Chicago City Basketball League, 19
Cooper, Charles "Tarzan," 4–5

Harlem Globetrotters, 15, 21–22
Harris, Lusia, 25
Henderson, Edwin B., 6–11

integration, 21–22
Interscholastic Athletic Association, 7

Naismith Memorial Basketball Hall of Fame, 5, 10, 17, 25
National Basketball Association (NBA), 5, 21–22, 25, 27
New York Renaissance, 4–5, 14, 19, 21

Posey, Cumberland, Jr., 16, 18

Roamer Girls, 19
Robinson, Jackie, 20, 22

segregation, 6–7

Washington, Ora, 17–18
Women's National Basketball Association (WNBA), 5, 22, 24, 27

PHOTO ACKNOWLEDGMENTS

Image credits: Cicely Lewis portrait photos by Fernando Decillis, p. 2; AP Photo/Charles Knoblock, p. 4; WorldPhotos/Alamy, pp. 5, 9, 12; Shawshots/Alamy, p. 6; Wikimedia Commons PD, p. 7 (top) (bottom); Schomburg Center for Research in Black Culture, Jean Blackwell Hutson Research and Reference Division, The New York Public Library/Getty Images, p. 8; Mike Zarrilli/Getty Images for Naismith Basketball Hall of Fame/Getty Images, p. 10; Charles 'Teenie' Harris/Carnegie Museum of Art/Getty Images, p. 11; Library of Congress, p. 13; Chicago History Museum/Getty Images, p. 15; Wikimedia Commons PD, p. 16; Courtesy of the Charles L. Blockson Afro-American Collection, Temple University Libraries, Philadelphia, Pennsylvania, p. 17; Science History Images/Alamy, p. 18; Charles 'Teenie' Harris/Carnegie Museum of Art/Getty Images, p. 20; Mark Rucker/Transcendental Graphics/Getty Images, p. 21 (left); AP Photo, p. 21 (right); AP Photo/Ed Ford, p. 22; Photo by Focus on Sport/Getty Images, p. 23; Photo by Walter Iooss Jr./Sports Illustrated/Getty Images, p. 24; John G. Zimmerman/Sports Illustrated/Getty Images, p. 25; AP Photo/Shaina Benhiyoun/SPP/Sipa USA, p. 26; Ronald Martinez/Getty Images, p. 27; Design Element: Sandipkumar Patel/Getty Images; Colors Hunter - Chasseur de Couleurs/Getty Images.

Cover: Courtesy of the Charles L. Blockson Afro-American Collection, Temple University Libraries, Philadelphia, Pennsylvania; AP Photo/Robert Kradin; Sandipkumar Patel/Getty Images; Colors Hunter - Chasseur de Couleurs/Getty Images.

Copyright © 2025 by Lerner Publishing Group, Inc.

All rights reserved. International copyright secured. No part of this book may be reproduced, stored in a retrieval system, or transmitted in any form or by any means—electronic, mechanical, photocopying, recording, or otherwise—without the prior written permission of Lerner Publishing Group, Inc., except for the inclusion of brief quotations in an acknowledged review.

Lerner Publications Company
An imprint of Lerner Publishing Group, Inc.
241 First Avenue North
Minneapolis, MN 55401 USA

For reading levels and more information, look up this title at www.lernerbooks.com.

Main body text set in Aptifer Sans LT Pro.
Typeface provided by Linotype AG.

Editor: Brianna Kaiser **Designer:** Viet Chu
Lerner team: Martha Kranes

Library of Congress Cataloging-in-Publication Data

Names: Smith, Elliott, author.
Title: Hoops heroes : the untold story of Black basketball / Elliott Smith.
Description: Minneapolis : Lerner Publications, 2025. | Series: Read woke books. Black trailblazers in sports | Includes bibliographical references and index. | Audience: Ages 9–14 | Audience: Grades 4–6 | Summary: "Black athletes had been playing basketball long before the NBA and WNBA existed. Discover basketball's origins, the stars of the Black Fives, and the Black Fives's lasting impact on the sport"— Provided by publisher.
Identifiers: LCCN 2023033973 (print) | LCCN 2023033974 (ebook) | ISBN 9798765611555 (library binding) | ISBN 9798765628515 (paperback) | ISBN 9798765632727 (epub)
Subjects: LCSH: Basketball—United States—History—Juvenile literature. | African American basketball players—History.
Classification: LCC GV885.1 .S594 2025 (print) | LCC GV885.1 (ebook) | DDC 796.323—dc23/eng/20230721

LC record available at https://lccn.loc.gov/2023033973
LC ebook record available at https://lccn.loc.gov/2023033974

Manufactured in the United States of America
1-1010005-51777-10/31/2023